TABLE OF CONTENTS

Synopsis 1

Author Information 2

Pre-Reading Activities 3

Chapters 1 - 3 . . . . 4 - 5

Chapters 4 - 5 . . . . 6 - 8

Chapters 8 - 10 . . . . 9 - 10

Chapters 11 - 13 . . . . 11 - 12

Chapters 14 - 16 . . . . 13 - 15

Chapters 17 - 19 . . . . 16 - 18

Chapters 20 - 22 . . . . 19 - 20

Chapters 23 - 25 . . . . 21 - 22

Chapters 26 - 28 . . . . 23 - 24

Chapters 29 - 33 . . . . 25 - 27

Cloze Activity 28

Post-Reading Activities. . . . . 29 - 30

Suggestions For Further Reading. 31

Answer Key . . . . 32 - 35

Notes 36

Novel-Ties® are printed on recycled paper.

For the Teacher

This reproducible study guide consists of lessons to use in conjunction with *The Yearling*. Written in chapter-by-chapter format, the guide contains a synopsis, pre-reading activities, vocabulary and comprehension exercises, as well as extension activities to be used as follow-up to the novel.

In a homogeneous classroom, whole class instruction with one title is appropriate. In a heterogeneous classroom, reading groups should be formed: each group works on a different novel at its reading level. Depending upon the length of time devoted to reading in the classroom, each novel, with its guide and accompanying lessons, may be completed in three to six weeks.

Begin using NOVEL-TIES for reading development by distributing the novel and a folder to each child. Distribute duplicated pages of the study guide for students to place in their folders. After examining the cover and glancing through the book, students can participate in several pre-reading activities. Vocabulary questions should be considered prior to reading a chapter; all other work should be done after the chapter has been read. Comprehension questions can be answered orally or in writing. The classroom teacher should determine the amount of work to be assigned, always keeping in mind that readers must be nurtured and that the ultimate goal is encouraging students' love of reading.

The benefits of using NOVEL-TIES are numerous. Students read good literature in the original, rather than in abridged or edited form. The good reading habits, formed by practice in focusing on interpretive comprehension and literary techniques, will be transferred to the books students read independently. Passive readers become active, avid readers.

SYNOPSIS

The Yearling is the story of twelve-year-old Jody Baxter and his coming of age in rural Florida in the 1870s. Although his family is poor, Jody's life is rich in experiences with nature. His father, Penny Baxter, having lost his other children in infancy, dotes on Jody, allowing him to enjoy his childhood, while Ma Baxter has been embittered by her loss. Besides his chores, Jody spends his time hunting with and visiting his friend Fodder-wing.

While he is on a bear hunt, Penny Baxter is bitten by a rattlesnake and kills a doe for its organs to sap the venom. Jody begs to keep the doe's orphaned fawn as a pet. Penny agrees, overruling Ma Baxter's complaints. Jody devotes himself to the fawn, whom he names Flag, giving him his own milk and part of his food. When wolves attack the livestock, Jody allows Flag to sleep in his bedroom. Ma Baxter silently disapproves.

When Penny is hurt uprooting a tree stump, Jody does the spring planting. To Penny's delight Jody works hard, even earning his mother's respect. But then Flag ruins the tobacco seedlings. Penny tells Jody to pen up the deer, who is now a full-grown yearling so that all of their crops will not be destroyed. Flag, however, escapes and attacks the corn sprouts. Jody fears Penny's reactions, but Penny agrees to let Jody build a fence around the field. Jody does the arduous work, helped unexpectedly by Ma Baxter.

Even then the field is not safe; Flag manages to hop over the fence and destroy the crop. Penny can no longer make excuses for the deer and he orders Jody to kill his pet. When Jody is unable to destroy the animal, Ma Baxter reluctantly shoots the deer, wounding him painfully. Jody is forced to complete the killing.

Devastated, Jody runs away, determined to stay with a friend of the family who is a sailor in Boston. After several days without food and heartsick about the things he has said to his father, Jody returns home. This experience has helped him understand Penny's decision about the deer and appreciate the love he and his father share.

BIOGRAPHICAL INFORMATION: Marjorie Kinnan Rawlings

Marjorie Kinnan Rawlings was born on August 8, 1896 in Washington, D.C. to Frank and Ida May Kinnan; a son was born a few years later. Marjorie's family spent summers in Maryland on the family farm where she took long walks with her father, to whom she was very close. From girlhood, Marjorie was sure that she would become a professional writer and at age eleven she won a $2.00 prize for a story which was published in *The Washington Post*.

After her graduation from high school at age seventeen, Marjorie's father died, a loss she would always feel. Her mother moved with the children to Madison, Wisconsin where Marjorie and her brother spent summers on her grandfather's farm. Marjorie attended the University of Wisconsin, majoring in English and editing the literary magazine. After graduating with honors in 1918, she moved to New York City where she worked on the editorial staff of the YWCA's National Board.

In 1919 she married her college sweetheart, Charles Rawlings, and moved to his hometown, Rochester, New York. Writing for a local newspaper was not exciting for Marjorie, but it taught her the important lessons of writing with clarity and simplicity.

Dissatisfied with city life, she and her husband bought an orange grove in the tiny north-central Florida community of Cross Creek. Marjorie loved the rural setting and she developed a great respect for its people. Here she began to write in the way she had always wanted. Her first story, "Cracker Chidlings" was sold to *Scribner's Magazine*; a few months later *Scribner's* also published "Jacob's Ladder." In 1933 Marjorie's story "Gal Young Un" won the O. Henry Memorial Award and her first novel, *South Moon Under*, was published.

In 1938 her work reached its zenith with the publication of *The Yearling*. To gather material for the novel, Marjorie went into the heart of the scrub country to learn about families who live there, going with them on bear hunts, and listening to the tales told by the older folk. Although its setting is Rawlings' beloved rural Florida, *The Yearling* has universal appeal as the story of a boy's troubled years as he grows from child to young man.

Because of *The Yearling*, Marjorie Kinnan Rawlings was elected to the National Academy of Arts and Letters in 1938 and was awarded the Pulitzer Prize in 1939. As she became a successful writer, her first marriage disintegrated and in 1941 she married Norton S. Baskin, moving with him to St. Augustine, Florida. There she published *Cross Creek* in 1942, the non-fiction account of her life in the rural Florida community she had come to regard as home. Its success was followed by two other books; one of them, *The Secret River*, was a runner-up for the Newbery Medal in 1956, three years after Marjorie Kinnan Rawlings' death in St. Augustine.

PRE-READING ACTIVITIES

1. Preview the book by reading the title and author's name and by looking at the cover illustration. What do you think the book will be about? Where and when does it take place? Have you read any other books by the same author?

2. HaTurn to the copyright page at the beginning of the book and notice the date of the first copyright. What qualities would make a book remain popular for so many years?

3. **Social Studies Connection:** Go online to do some research about the community of Cross Creek, Florida, the place where Marjorie Kinnan Rawlings lived most of her adult life and wrote *The Yearling*. Find pictures of Cross Creek in the 1930s and today. As you read *The Yearling* compare today's Cross Creek with the earlier one described in the book.

4. Do you own a pet? Do you take responsibility for any of its care? Describe what you do for it. Has it ever misbehaved and caused trouble in the family? How was this situation resolved? If you do not have a pet, describe the kind of pet you might want to have. What kind of care would you provide for it? What problems might be caused by having this pet in your family? How would you deal with these problems?

5. Have you ever felt ignored and misunderstood by your parents? Why did this occur? Was this problem resolved?

6. What jobs or chores are you responsible for at home? How important are your chores? Is it ever permissible to skip them? When must they be done?

7. Do you have a job? If so, how do you feel about the responsibility it entails? If you don't have one now, what kind of job would you like to have?

8. What does being a good neighbor mean? Have you ever experienced a crisis where neighbors helped each other? Are neighbors more or less important to each other in a rural area than in an urban one? Why?

9. Do you feel that one parent, relative, or other adult understands you better than any other person? Can you discuss things with this person that would otherwise remain private? In order to provide realism in her novel, Marjorie Kinnan Rawlings writes the words of the characters in the informal language or dialect of rural Florida. Choose a passage from the beginning of the book and translate the dialect into standard American English. How can dialect contribute to the flavor of a story?

CHAPTERS 1 - 3

Vocabulary: Draw a line from each word on the left to its definition on the right. Then use the numbered words to fill in the blanks in the sentences below.

1.	fragile	a.	having delicate health; weak
2.	dense	b.	deep and painful regret for wrongdoing
3.	frail	c.	crowded or compact
4.	stern	d.	deliberate destruction of property
5.	adjacent	e.	adjoining; neighboring
6.	arid	f.	being without moisture
7.	vandalism	g.	easily broken; shattered
8.	remorse	h.	strict; firm

. . . .

1. The children were punished for their _____ by being required to clean up the school grounds.

2. The smile on the criminal's face showed that he had no _____ for his crime.

3. The crystal glasses are too _____ to withstand shipping.

4. High temperatures do not seem so bad in a(n) _____ desert environment.

5. A lengthy illness made my grandmother seem _____ and tired.

6. The judge issued a(n) _____ warning to the jury that they must not discuss their case.

7. Even though it was a sunny morning, it seemed like dusk as we walked through the _____ forest.

8. The family living in the apartment _____ to mine were so noisy that I could not sleep last night.

Questions:

1. Why did Jody go to the Glen? What evidence showed that Jody was very happy in this place?

2. How did Jody's father react when Jody returned from the Glen? Why didn't Jody's father tell his wife that Jody had been away from the farm?

Chapters 1 - 3 (cont.)

3. How did Jody's mother react when she learned that Jody had gone to the Glen?

4. Why had Penny Baxter settled on Pine Island?

5. Why did Jody feel justified in hunting old Slewfoot with his dad?

Questions for Discussion:

1. How do you know that Jody's family was poor?

2. What kind of relationship did Jody have with each of his parents? Why had this relationship evolved?

Literary Devices:

I. *Simile* — A simile is a figure of speech in which two unlike objects are compared using the words "like" or "as." For example:

> Small clouds were stationary, like balls of cotton.

What is being compared? What visual image does this simile create?

_____

_____

II. *Personification* — Personification in literature refers to the granting of human qualities to non-living objects. For example:

> The dusky glen laid cool hands on him.

What is being personified? What mood does this create?

_____

_____

Literary Element: Setting

Setting refers to the time and place where the events of a story occur. What is the setting of this story? How do you know that the setting is an important element in this story?

Writing Activity:

Reread those parts of Chapter One that refer to setting. Notice how the author's choice of words helps you visualize the places described. Choose a setting that is familiar to you and write about it using descriptive language.

CHAPTERS 4 - 7

Vocabulary: Synonyms are words with similar meanings. Draw a line from each word in column A to its synonym in column B. Then use the words in column A to fill in the blanks in the sentences below.

<u>A</u>   <u>B</u>

1. precarious   a. offspring
2. progeny   b. insult
3. wary   c. useless
4. obstruction   d. jutted
5. futile   e. cautious
6. disconsolate   f. dangerous
7. offend   g. impediment
8. protruded   h. heartbroken

. . . .

1. The children were _____ when their beloved dog died.

2. A stalled truck became a(n) _____ to all westward moving traffic.

3. The mare proudly displayed her newborn _____ who walked beside her on wobbly legs.

4. The class was given lessons in good manners so that their behavior would not _____ their visitors.

5. The tightrope walker seemed to ignore his _____ position as he moved gracefully high above the crowd.

6. Once we added extra pieces to the dining room table, it _____ into the living room.

7. The infant struggled for a long time before realizing it was _____ to try to fit the round peg into a square hole.

8. Sailors were warned to be _____ of high winds during the approaching storm.

Chapters 4 - 7 (cont.)

Questions:

1. Why was the loss of the brood sow a serious problem for Jody's family?

2. How did Penny track the bear?

3. Why wasn't Penny able to kill the bear?

4. Why did Penny need to go to the Forresters' farm? Why was Jody happy to accompany him?

5. Why was Jody excited about having a meal with the Forresters? Why do you think Penny seemed very grave by contrast?

6. How did Penny trick Lem Forrester into making a trade?

Questions for Discussion:

1. Do you approve of hunting? Do you agree or disagree with Penny's rationale for hunting?

2. Why did Penny consider his father "the core of safety"?

3. Why do you think Jody befriended Fodder-wing?

4. Do you think Penny took unfair advantage of Lem Forrester?

Literary Device: Metaphor

A metaphor is a figure of speech in which a comparison between two unlike objects is suggested or implied. For example:

> The bear was a black hurricane.

What is being compared?

_____

What visual image does this metaphor create?

_____

_____

Social Studies Connection:

Do some research to find out about the early Spanish explorers who traveled across Florida in search of gold and other valuable plunder.

Chapters 4 - 7 (cont.)

Literary Element: Characterization

Use the Venn diagram below to compare and contrast the Baxters and the Forresters.

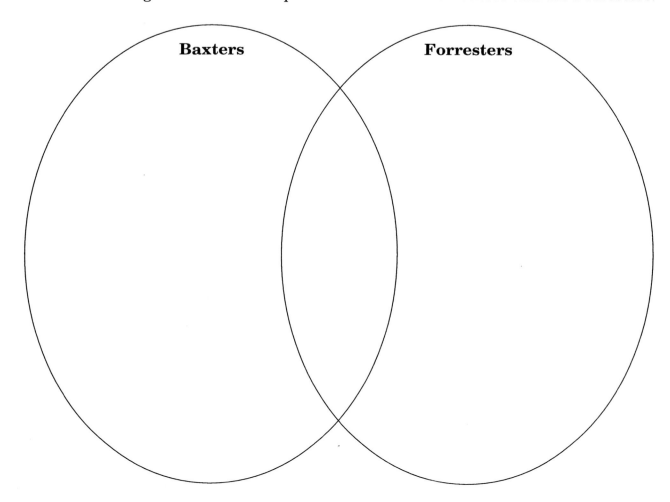

Baxters   **Forresters**

Writing Activity:

Write about a real or imaginary time when you or someone you know was the object of trickery.

CHAPTERS 8 - 10

Vocabulary: Antonyms are words with opposite meanings. Draw a line from each word in column A to its antonym in column B. Then use each word in column A to fill in the blanks in the sentences below.

	A		B
1.	bountiful	a.	race
2.	mollified	b.	convex
3.	luminous	c.	energetic
4.	tart	d.	loose
5.	languid	e.	scarce
6.	concave	f.	sweet
7.	taut	g.	dull
8.	amble	h.	provoked

. . . .

1. We added sugar to the lemonade so that it would not be too _____.

2. On a beautiful spring day, I love to _____ through the park and look at the flowers in bloom.

3. Water collected in the portion of the roof that had become _____ as it settled.

4. The moon was a(n) _____ sphere in the night sky.

5. After months of hard work, the farmers were grateful for a(n) _____ harvest.

6. The fishing line became _____ in the boy's hands, revealing that a fish was stuck on the hook.

7. The teacher's anger was _____ by her students' written apology for their bad behavior.

8. It was peaceful sitting beside the _____ pond where our thoughts were never disturbed by a ripple or a splash.

Questions:

1. Why did Jody feel resentment mixed with pleasure when he returned home from the Forresters?

2. What was Jody's greatest wish? Why didn't his father think he could satisfy that wish?

Chapters 8 - 10 (cont.)

3. How did Jody's mother treat his illness? Why do you think she did not take Jody to a doctor?

4. How did Penny show his respect for the ecology of the freshwater pond?

Questions for Discussion:

1. Why do you think Ma treated Jody so gruffly?

2. How would you explain Jody's ability to love the chase, hate the kill, and still enjoy the meat?

3. How did Jody approach his farm tasks? Do you think he was lazy?

Science Connection:

Reread part of Chapter Nine and do some additional research to learn how underground rivers may cause sink holes. Also learn more about how sedimentary rock, such as limestone, is formed.

Social Studies Connection:

How would you describe the division of labor between Ma and Pa Baxter? How does it compare to the division of labor between men and women in families today?

Writing Activities:

1. Jody found that "whenever he had been away . . . and came home again, he noticed things that he had never noticed before." Write about a time when you returned to a familiar place and noticed things you never saw before.

2. Reread the description of the dancing cranes in Chapter Ten. Notice how the author used short, deceptively simple sentences to describe the scene. Using her description as a model, write about a scene you have observed.

CHAPTERS 11 - 13

Vocabulary: Analogies are equations in which the first pair of words has the same relationship as the second pair of words. For example: TRUE is to FALSE as DAWN is to DUSK. Both pairs of words are opposites. Choose the best word from the Word Box to complete each of the analogies below.

WORD BOX			
itinerant	menace	puny	tumult
keen	precede	sedate	venom

1. FRIEND is to COMRADE as COMMOTION is to _____.
2. SKUNK is to SPRAY as SNAKE is to _____.
3. CONTENT is to UNHAPPY as _____ is to FOLLOW.
4. CALM is to TURBULENT as SETTLED is to _____.
5. HEALTHY is to ROBUST as WEAK is to _____.
6. WATER is to RESTORATIVE as POLLUTION is to _____.
7. DULL is to _____ as SULLEN is to JOYOUS.
8. AGITATED is to·EXCITED as _____ is to SERENE.

Questions:
1. Why did Penny take Jody with him on the hunting trip that would end in Volusia?
2. How did Jody react to the deer he and Penny shot?
3. What was the role of the storekeeper in his community?
4. Why did Jody feel so comfortable at Grandma Hutto's cabin?
5. Why was there such excitement when Oliver came home?
6. Why did Jody regret participating in the fight against Lem Forrester?

Questions for Discussion:
1. Do you agree with Grandma Hutto's assessment of Jody's mother? Why do you think Ma Baxter might be so stern?
2. Do you think Jody had some part in instigating the fight between Oliver and Lem?
3. Do you think Fodder-wing will not change as Jody predicted?
4. How do you think Jody's mother will react when she sees her son and husband again?

Chapters 11 - 13 (cont.)

Literary Devices:

I. *Personification* — What is personified in the following passage:

> It [the St. John's River] seemed to slide toward the ocean indifferent to its own banks and to the men who crossed or used it.

What visual image does this create?

_____

_____

II. *Metaphor* — What is being compared in the following passage:

> Grandma Hutto's flower garden was a bright patchwork quilt thrown down inside the pickets.

Why is this better than saying, "Grandma had a colorful flower garden in her front yard"?

_____

_____

_____

Social Studies Connection:

Do some research to find out how the Civil War affected Florida and the people who lived there, such as Grandma Hutto. Also, learn about the Battle of Bull Run where Yankees such as Easy were beaten.

Writing Activity:

Imagine you are Jody and that you had learned to write. Write a journal entry on the day after the fight. Describe the fight and your complex feelings about it.

CHAPTERS 14 - 16

Vocabulary: Use the context to determine the meaning of the underlined word in each of the following sentences. Circle the letter of the definition you choose.

1. The farmers erected a wire fence around the pasture to protect the livestock against the <u>intrusion</u> of wild animals.

    a. legal act   b. wrongful act   c. rapid departure d. herding
       of entering   of entering

2. The boy felt <u>incompetent</u> when he tried unsuccessfully to light a fire by rubbing flint against stone.

    a. lacking   b. qualified   c. grateful   d. lacking ability
       intelligence

3. The tired hikers seemed more <u>amiable</u> in each other's company once they had a meal and a bath.

    a. friendly   b. challenged   c. weary   d. hostile

4. The family knew it would be difficult to make their currently <u>barren</u> land produce a cash crop.

    a. unproductive   b. fertile   c. vast   d. plowed

5. If you want to protect the chicken coop against raiding raccoons and foxes, you will need to keep an all-night <u>vigil</u>.

    a. slumber   b. feast   c. parade   d. watch

6. After two months without rain, the farmers were <u>delirious</u> with joy when the first drops wet their backs.

    a. content   b. ecstatic   c. depressed   d. puzzled

Questions:

1. Why did Ma encourage Jody and his father to go out again on a hunt? Why wasn't she concerned about an encounter with the Forresters?
2. Why did Penny shoot the deer even though it had a fawn?
3. Why did Jody and Ma consider Buck Forrester a friend?
4. Why was Jody able to get parental permission to have a fawn?
5. When did Buck decide it was time to return home?
6. How did the Baxters get a bear?

Chapters 14 - 16 (cont.)

Questions for Discussion:

1. What do you think was responsible for saving Penny Baxter's life?

2. Why do you think Buck was willing to live and work so hard at the Baxters' farm? What did he accomplish while he was there?

Literary Devices:

I. *Simile* — What is being compared in the following simile:

   The air lay over the road like a thick down comforter.

   _____

   What visual image does this create?

   _____

   _____

II. *Personification* — What is personified in the following passage:

   The sunrise reached long fingers into the clearing.

   _____

   What visual image does this create?

   _____

   _____

Science Connection

Do some research on rattlesnakes. Learn about their habits, where they live, and how they protect themselves. Also, find out about antidotes to the poison of their bites.

Author's Style:

Reread the portion of Chapter Fourteen where Jody is returning to the cabin. How does the author build suspense over Penny's condition?

_____

_____

_____

_____

Chapters 14 - 16 (cont.)

Literary Element: Characterization

Use the Venn diagram below to compare Ma Baxter with her foil, Grandma Hutto. Show how they are alike in the overlapping section of the circles.

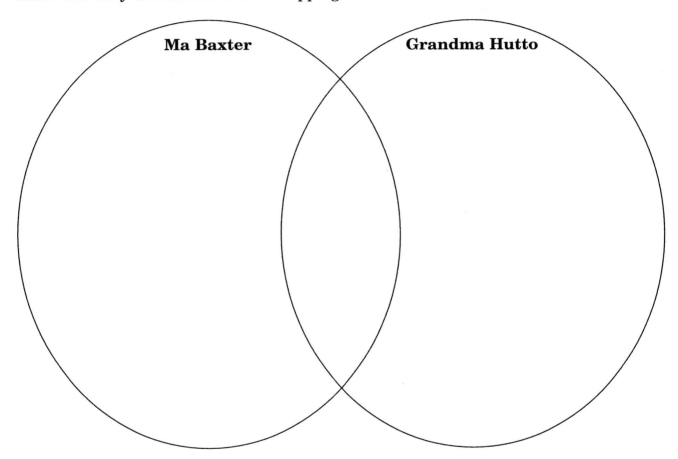

Writing Activity:

Imagine you are Jody and write about the day Buck shot the bear. Tell about your father's recovery and what life might be like when Buck leaves.

CHAPTERS 17 - 19

Vocabulary: Use the words in the Word Box and the clues below to complete the crossword puzzle.

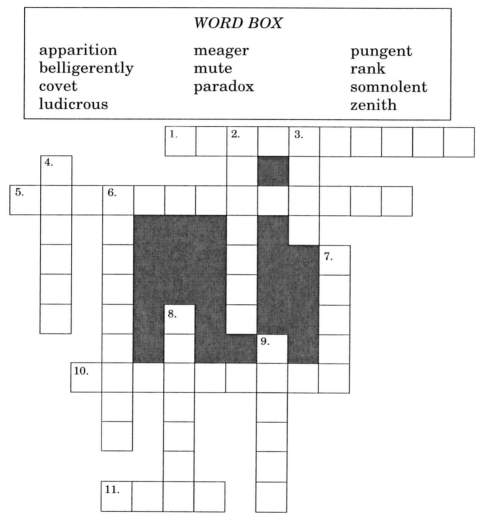

WORD BOX

apparition	meager	pungent
belligerently	mute	rank
covet	paradox	somnolent
ludicrous		zenith

Across

1. ghost
5. in a quarrelsome manner
10. drowsy
11. silent

Down

2. puzzle
3. disgusting
4. highest point; summit
6. causing laughter because of absurdity
7. envy
8. sharply affecting the senses of smell or taste
9. lacking in quantity or quality

Chapters 17 - 19 (cont.)

Questions:

1. How did Penny's recuperation from the snake bite affect his son Jody?

2. Why did Jody feel privileged to have seen the two male bears fighting?

3. How did Jody react to Fodder-wing's death? Why did Jody spend the night with the Baxters on the night of Fodder-wing's death?

4. Why did Penny's presence provide comfort to the Baxters?

5. What was the Forresters' peace offering to the Baxters?

6. What fear did Penny's hunting story evoke in Jody? How did Penny try to allay his son's fears?

7. How did the eight-day storm affect the Baxters and their farm?

Questions for Discussion:

1. Do you think Ma's tolerance of the fawn suggested her approval of the animal? Why did she tolerate the animal?

2. How would you assess Penny's eulogy at Fodder-wing's burial? Do you think his words were appropriate, or should he have spoken differently?

3. Why do you think Jody was disappointed when he realized that Fodder-wing's Spaniard was an illusion?

4. Is your life controlled by the climate in any ways that are similar to Jody's experience?

5. How would you assess Jody's relationship with Flag? Should a person and his pet be so close?

Literary Devices:

I. *Metaphor* — What is being compared in the following metaphor:

> They [the Forresters] were pieces of one great dark rock, broken into separate men.

_____

Why is this such an apt comparison?

_____

_____

Chapters 17 - 19 (cont.)

II. *Allusion* — Allusion is a reference in literature to a familiar person, place, or event. Why did Penny allude to the biblical tale of Noah? Was this an apt allusion?

_____

_____

Author's Style:

Reread the author's description of the two male bears in Chapter Seventeen. In the chart below, write those phrases that the author used to elicit the senses of sight, sound, smell, and touch.

Sight	
Sound	
Smell	
Touch	

Writing Activity:

Notice how the author grants importance to the changing of the seasons. Write about the ways the changing seasons affect you and the people in your environment.

CHAPTERS 20 - 22

Vocabulary: Draw a line from each word on the left to its definition on the right. Then use the numbered words to fill in the blanks in the sentences below.

1. palatable   a. come upon or meet with

2. unprecedented   b. having an unpleasant odor

3. encounter   c. tasty; savory

4. transparent   d. lack of the usual comforts of life

5. sodden   e. shelter; protection from danger

6. malodorous   f. soaked with liquid

7. refuge   g. clear; easily seen through

8. privation   h. never known before or experienced

. . . .

1. The campers sought _____ in their tents once the storm began.

2. Our clothes became _____ after we walked for hours in the rain.

3. The _____ amount of snow in our area caused all means of transportation to shut down.

4. After months of _____, all of the animals appeared weak and tired.

5. We put ketchup on the meat to make it more _____.

6. After my _____ with a wildcat in the woods, I took extra care on all future walks.

7. Do not drink the water from the _____ pond, since the odor suggests a bad water supply.

8. Once they were cleaned, sun poured through the _____ windows.

Questions:

1. Why did Buck and Mill-wheel Forrester go off together with Penny and Jody? Why wouldn't Penny allow Jody to take the fawn along?

2. How did Penny's feelings about hunting differ from that of the Forresters? Do you agree with Penny or the Forresters?

3. How did the storm affect the land?

Chapters 20 - 22 (cont.)

4. Why was Jody able to shoot a bear?

5. Why were so many animals dying after the storm ended? What implications did this have for Jody and his fawn? What implications did this have for the Baxters?

6. Why did the Baxters kill their own hogs?

7. Why did Jody's parents take the fawn's actions so seriously?

Questions for Discussion:

1. Why did Jody and the Forresters enjoy Penny's tales about the past? Do you enjoy hearing adults recount stories about events they experienced or those that were handed down to them?

2. Do you think Jody's feelings about hunting changed after he shot the bear?

3. Do you agree with Penny that considerations about food must come before considerations about the fawn?

Writing Activity:

On the night of the campfire, Jody wished time would stand still and he could always camp like that. Write about a real or imagined time that was so perfect for you that you wished time could stand still.

CHAPTERS 23 - 25

Vocabulary: Use the context to figure out the meaning of the underlined word in each of the following sentences. Circle the letter of the word or phrase you choose.

1. The writer was <u>elated</u> when his work was chosen for publication.

   a. depressed b. puzzled c. overjoyed d. disturbed

2. The prisoners became <u>emaciated</u> on a diet of watery soup and gruel.

   a. obese b. thin c. radiant d. nervous

3. When you are tired and weak, you become <u>vulnerable</u> to disease.

   a. off-limits b. fascinating c. immune d. open to attack

4. Using a clever <u>ruse</u>, the detectives got the suspect to admit his guilt.

   a. trick b. alibi c. melody d. costume

5. Everyone wondered how the young mother could smile <u>complacently</u> while her infant played near the water's edge.

   a. tragically b. sincerely c. smugly d. foolishly

6. The spectators in the stands became restless during the long <u>interval</u> between the first race and the second.

   a. pause b. band show c. television program d. rest

7. As the only <u>legitimate</u> child, Charles knew that he alone would inherit his father's fortune.

   a. youthful b. affectionate c. educated d. lawful

8. The <u>timorous</u> driver will not be able to get through midtown city traffic.

   a. aggressive b. cowardly c. rude d. limousine

Questions:

1. Why were the wolves a continuing threat to the Baxter farm?
2. How did Penny and the Forresters disagree about the wolves? Who do you think is right?
3. Why was Jody angry at Oliver Hutto?
4. Why did the Forresters relent and agree to hunt the remaining wolves?

Chapters 23 - 25 (cont.)

5. What animals best survived the plague?

6. Why did the Baxter family make a trip by wagon to Volusia? Why did they consider this a special excursion?

Questions for Discussion:

1. Reread the list of goods Penny and Ma gave to Buck as trade for the bears. Which items do you think were necessities and which were luxuries? How does the Baxters' idea of luxury differ from your own?

2. Do you think Jody was paying too much attention to the fawn and its needs?

Literary Devices:

I. *Symbolism* — A symbol in literature is a person, an object, or an event that represents an idea or a set of ideas. What do you think Fodder-wing's Spaniard symbolizes?

II. *Irony* — Dramatic irony, a device usually used in the theater, refers to a character's mistakes which are understood by the audience, but not by the character. What was ironic about Ma Baxter's pronouncement to Jody, "You best study your grammar . . . you'd ought to say, 'the roaches has eat it.'"

III. *Metaphor* — What is being compared in the following metaphor? What mood does it create?

> The sun was a warm arm across their shoulders.

Science Connection:

Do some research to learn about wolves. What are their preferred habitats, what do they eat, how would you characterize their behavior, and what is their degree of intelligence? Find out whether they have become endangered.

Writing Activity:

Write about a time when you felt the kind of anxiety Jody experienced when he feared a return of the wolf pack. Describe the situation, using as much descriptive language as possible.

CHAPTERS 26 - 28

Vocabulary: Analogies are equations in which the first pair of words has the same relationship as the second pair of words. For example: COMIC is to TRAGIC as COSTLY is to CHEAP. Both pairs of words are opposites. Choose the best word from the Word Box to complete each of the analogies below.

```
                          WORD BOX

        boisterous    imperceptible   jovial          whimper
        harbinger     impetus         lethargy
```

1. REFUGE is to SHELTER as FORERUNNER is to _____.

2. COMMENCE is to CONCLUDE as _____ is to CALM.

3. CHUCKLE is to LAUGH as _____ is to SOB.

4. OBVIOUS is to _____ as OBESE is to SLENDER.

5. BOOST is to _____ as EXUBERANCE is to ENTHUSIASM.

6. COLD is to ACTION as HEAT is to _____.

7. FROWN is to ANGRY as SMILE is to _____.

Questions:

1. How did Jody's mother react to the gift of the black alpaca? Why do you think she reacted this way?

2. Why didn't Penny think he would be able to attend Christmas celebrations in Volusia? Why was Ma Baxter particularly disappointed?

3. Why wasn't Penny able to shoot down the bear when he first spotted him?

4. How did Nellie Ginright make the rest of the bear hunt easier for Penny and Jody?

5. How did the Forresters come to Penny and Jody's aid?

6. How were Penny and Jody treated when they arrived at the church in Volusia?

Chapters 26 - 28 (cont.)

Questions for Discussion:

1. Do you think Penny should have gone with his family to Volusia instead of going on the bear hunt?

2. Why do you think the author described the Forresters practical joke and their behavior at the Christmas festivities just before Grandma Hutto's house burned?

3. What might have happened if Grandma Hutto had not told Oliver that she started the fire by accident?

4. Why do you think Grandma Hutto decided to leave Volusia for Boston?

5. Why did Jody equate the Hutto's departure with their death?

Writing Activity:

Imagine you are a newspaper reporter and write an article describing the events in Volusia on Christmas Eve. Be sure to include the critical *who, what, where, when,* and *why* in the first paragraph.

CHAPTERS 29 - 33

Vocabulary: Draw a line from each word on the left to its meaning on the right. Then use the numbered words to fill in the blanks in the sentences below.

1.	lamented	a.	exhausting; hard
2.	melancholy	b.	loud, confused noise
3.	impudent	c.	persuaded by flattery or promises
4.	plausible	d.	stimulus; encouragement
5.	arduous	e.	rude
6.	incentive	f.	expressed sorrow or regret for
7.	din	g.	sadness; dejection
8.	cajoled	h.	having an appearance of truth

. . . .

1. No matter how much the boy _____ his parents, they would not let him have a motorcycle.

2. Even with the help of machinery, planting a crop is _____ work.

3. The children became _____ when their beloved pet died.

4. Money is often the _____ for hard work.

5. When Sally moved far away, I _____ the loss of a very good friend.

6. It was impossible to hear your voice over the _____ of the orchestra tuning up.

7. The child was punished for his _____ behavior.

8. Only a(n) _____ explanation will excuse you from this homework assignment.

Idioms:

Idioms are phrases which are characteristic of a particular region of a country or a group of people. They contain words which are part of the language but are used in a way that is different from ordinary speech, for example: "shake a leg" means hurry up. Below is a list of idioms which are found in *The Yearling*. Write what each one means in your own words.

1. "You cain't get all your 'coons up one tree."

_____

Chapters 29 - 33 (cont.)

2. "The fiddle cain't play without the bow."

_____

3. ". . . a toad-strangler of a rain. . ."

_____

4. "Now you know," Penny said, "the same dog bit me."

_____

5. ". . . Jody was too rattle-headed."

_____

6. "Her and me don't never swap much honey."

_____

Questions:

1. How had Flag's behavior changed as he became a yearling?
2. Why was Flag's destruction of the seed bed a serious matter?
3. Why was Jody relieved after his parents' first conference about Flag and the cornfield?
4. What made Jody's parents reverse their decision about Flag? How do you know it was particularly difficult for Penny to reach this conclusion?
5. How did the Forresters disappoint Jody?
6. Why did Jody blame his father after Flag died?
7. How did Jody learn the real meaning of hunger and come to understand his parents' fear of hunger?
8. What motivated Jody to rush home?

Questions for Discussion:

1. What do you think Penny was thinking when he looked at his son and Flag and said, "You're a pair o' yearlin's . . . Hit grieves me"?
2. Do you think that Penny should have been stricter with Jody and less tolerant of the fawn?
3. Do you think there was any other solution to the Baxters' problem than to shoot Flag?

Chapters 29 - 33 (cont.)

4.   Who do you think was responsible for Flag's death?

5.   What do you think Penny meant when he told Jody he had changed, that he was no longer a yearling?

Literary Devices:

I.   *Foreshadowing* — Foreshadowing in literature refers to the clues an author provides to suggest what will happen later in a story. What events foreshadowed Flag's death?

_____

_____

II.   *Symbolism* — What did the flutter-mill symbolize to Jody? Why didn't the new one satisfy him?

_____

_____

Literary Element: Theme

A theme in a work of literature is its central idea or message. One important theme in *The Yearling* is growing up or coming of age. How has the author made this theme central to the novel? What messages has the author given about reaching maturity?

Writing Activities:

1.   Write about a real or imagined time when you felt that you needed to run away from home. Describe the situation that made you want to leave and tell what happened.

2.   Write about a time when you felt as Jody did in the following passage:

> He hung suspended in a timeless space. He could go neither forward nor back. Something was ended. Nothing was begun.

CLOZE ACTIVITY

The following excerpt is taken from Chapter Fifteen of the novel. Read it through completely and then go back and fill in the blank spaces with words that make sense. When you finish, you may compare your language with that of the author.

He remembered his father's saying that a fawn would follow that had been first carried. He started away slowly. The fawn _____[1] after him. He came back to _____[2] and stroked it and walked away _____.[3] It took a few wobbling steps _____[4] him and cried piteously. It was _____[5] to follow him. It belonged to _____.[6] It was his own. He was light-headed _____[7] his joy. He wanted to fondle _____,[8] to run and romp with it, _____[9] call it to come to _____.[10] He dared not alarm it. He _____[11] it up and carried it in _____[12] of him over his two arms. _____[13] seemed to him that he walked _____[14] effort. He had the strength of _____[15] Forrester.

His arms began to ache and _____[16] was forced to stop again. When _____[17] walked on, the fawn followed him _____[18] once. He allowed it to walk _____[19] little distance, then picked it up _____.[20] The distance home was nothing. He could have walked all day and into the night, carrying it and watching it follow.

POST-READING ACTIVITIES

1. *The Yearling* took place in a rural setting where nature determined many aspects of the characters' lives. Discuss three incidents in the novel where the characters were at the mercy of nature.

2. Although the land was difficult to live on, Penny had chosen to live with his family in the Florida scrub country where he felt that "The peace of the vast aloof scrub had drawn him with the beneficence of its silence. Something in him was raw and tender. The touch of men was hurtful upon it, but the touch of the pines was healing. . . . The wild animals seemed less predatory to him than people he had known." Discuss whether or not you agree with Penny and support your answer with specific facts from the novel and your own experience.

3. Throughout the novel the values of the Forresters were contrasted with the values of the Baxters. Discuss the following topics and give the different attitudes toward them. In each instance tell whose point of view you agree with and why.

    *   the purpose of hunting
    *   telling the truth in trading
    *   killing wildcats after the flood
    *   proper behavior at a public gathering

4. Ma Baxter was portrayed as begrudging things that were fun for Jody and resenting the sharing of food. Marjorie Kinnan Rawlings said of her ". . . the going of too many of her children had wrung her dry of feeling. . . ." Do you think this statement explained her behavior? Do you think she loved Jody as much as Penny did? What incidents from the novel support your answer?

5. Death is a familiar figure in *The Yearling*. Describe how Fodder-wing's death affected Jody. How did Jody finally come to terms with his friend's death after seeing the raccoon family in the woods? How did this experience help Jody to accept the necessity of Flag's death?

6. Which character was hurt more by Flag's death—Jody or Penny? Support your answer with references from the novel.

7. **Art Connection:** The setting plays an especially important role in this book. The seasons change, nature provides high drama, and the characters react to the setting. Choose a scene that appeals to you and either draw a mural or construct a diorama based on a careful rereading of that section of the book.

Post-Reading Activities (cont.)

8. Choose a scene of dramatic action such as the fire, a bear hunt, or the Christmas "doings." Write a script for your scene and select appropriate music to accompany it. Dramatize your scene and, if possible, video tape it to present to the class.

9. **Science Connection:** Nature is constantly referred to in this book. List either the animals or plants that are mentioned. Then choose at least five to study. As part of your research, find out about the habitats, growing conditions, and important characteristics of the five you chose.

10. Most people who read *The Yearling* become emotionally involved with the characters. What language lends itself to this emotional involvement? Is it sympathy for a particular character? Why does the reader care about this character? How does the author avoid sentimentality?

11. View the video *Cross Creek*, which reveals Marjorie Kinnan Rawlings' beginnings as a writer. Afterwards, discuss with your classmates how her experiences and the place she lived affected her writing.

12. **Literature Circle:** Have a literature circle discussion in which you tell your personal reactions to *The Yearling*. Here are some questions and sentence starters to help your literature circle begin a discussion.

    - Compare yourself to one of the characters in the book. How aree you alike? How are you different?
    - Do any of the characters remind you of people that you know?
    - Do you find the characters in the novel realistic? Why or why not?
    - Which character do you like the most? The least?
    - What did you like best about this book? What did you like least?
    - Who else would you like to read this novel? Why?
    - What questions would you like to ask the author about this novel?
    - I was worried when . . .
    - I was pleased when . . .
    - I laughed when . . .
    - I would have liked to see . . .
    - I wonder . . .
    - Jody learned that . . .
    - I learned that . . .

SUGGESTIONS FOR FURTHER READING

* Armstrong, W.H. *Sounder*. HarperCollins.

* George, Jean. *My Side of the Mountain*. Puffin.

* Gipson, Fred. *Old Yeller*. HarperCollins.

Herriot, James. *All Creatures Great and Small*. St. Martin's Press.

_____. *James Herriot's Dog Stories*. St. Martin's Press.

Kjelgaard, Jim. *Big Red*. Yearling.

* Naylor, Phyllis Reynolds. *Shiloh*. Scholastic.

* North, Sterling. *Rascal*. Puffin.

* Paterson, Katherine. *Bridge to Terabithia*. HarperCollins.

* Rawls, Wilson. *Where the Red Fern Grows*. Yearling.

* Schaefer, Jack. *Shane*. Bantam.

* Steinbeck, John. *The Red Pony*. Penguin.

* Twain, Mark. *Adventures of Tom Sawyer*. Bantam.

* Wilder, Laura Ingalls. *Little House in the Big Woods*. HarperCollins.

* _____. *Little House on the Prairie*. HarperCollins.

Other Books by Marjorie Kinnan Rawlings

Cross Creek. Scribner.

Cross Creek Cookery. Fireside.

The Secret River. Canongate U.S.

The Sojourner. Berg.

South Moon Under. Amereon.

When the Whippoorwill. Ballantine.

* NOVEL-TIES Study Guides are available for these titles.

ANSWER KEY

Chapters 1-3

Vocabulary: 1. g 2. c 3. a 4. h 5. e 6. f 7. d 8. b; 1. vandalism 2. remorse 3. fragile 4. arid 5. frail 6. stern 7. dense 8. adjacent

Questions: 1. Jody went to the Glen because he seemed to be dissatisfied with his farm chores and wanted to go to his beautiful, special, secret place. Jody was so relaxed and happy when he got to the Glen that he was able to nap peacefully. When he awoke, he displayed his great happiness by whirling around. 2. Jody's father was not annoyed at Jody for neglecting his farm chores and going rambling on a spring day. He attributed this to youth. He also knew that his wife would not agree, so he decided to keep his son's ramblings a secret from her. In every way, he wanted to protect Jody from his wife's sharpness. 3. When Jody slipped and revealed he had been to the Glen, his mother surprised him by accepting his exploits and did not scold him for neglecting his chores. 4. Penny Baxter was a man of such character and unflinching honesty, that he had to live far from the relative dishonesty of the city to live in peace. 5. Jody was eager to hunt the grizzly because it had killed their brood sow and the family could eat its meat.

Chapters 4-7

Vocabulary: 1. f 2. a 3. e 4. g 5. c 6. h 7. b 8. d; 1. disconsolate 2. obstruction 3. progeny 4. offend 5. precarious 6. protruded 7. futile 8. wary

Questions: 1. The loss of the brood sow was tragic for Jody's family because they had counted on the sow's offspring as a source of food. 2. Penny used his knowledge of animal behavior and the bear's pawprints to lead him to the animal. His three hunting dogs picked up the scent and led the way. Penny also noticed signs of the bear's flight in fire-plants that were eaten along the way. 3. Penny was unable to kill the bear because his old gun did not fire properly. 4. Since Penny had no money to buy a new gun, he thought he would be able to trade the pup Feist. Jody was eager to go along because he would be able to visit his friend Fodder-wing. 5. Jody was excited to have a luxurious meal of venison and pudding, etc., that was so unlike his meager meals at home. Answers to the second part of the question will vary, but may include the idea that Penny felt envious of his neighbors and wondered whether he was a good enough provider for his small family. 6. Penny gave the impression that Feist was such a valuable dog that Lem would do anything to obtain him, even trade the dog for a gun.

Chapters 8-10

Vocabulary: 1. e 2. h 3. g 4. f 5. c 6. b 7. d 8. a; 1. tart 2. amble 3. concave 4. luminous 5. bountiful 6. taut 7. mollified 8. languid

Questions: 1. Jody was pleased that there was meat for the household, but resentful that he had missed the hunt. 2. More than anything, Jody wanted an animal to tame and have for a pet. Pa didn't think his wife would approve of such an impractical idea. 3. Jody's mother had a specific herbal remedy for each kind of illness she thought he had. While he seemed ill, she insisted on total bed rest. Answers to the second part of the question will vary, but should include the idea that doctors were rare, expensive, and only resorted to in times of dire emergencies. 4. Once Jody had caught a ten-pound bass that would be their supper, Penny insisted that all subsequent smaller fish they caught be thrown back.

Chapters 11-13

Vocabulary: 1. tumult 2. venom 3. precede 4. itinerant 5. puny 6. menace 7. keen 8. sedate

Questions: 1. Penny wanted Jody to accompany him because he wanted him to learn how to hunt and he enjoyed his son's company. 2. Jody was saddened when he saw the animal they shot. He wished they could obtain meat or make a trade without killing. 3. The storekeeper not only traded in important commodities, but he also acted as a judge and referee in disputes and was a dispenser of information. 4. Jody felt more at home at Grandma Hutto's cabin than he did at his own house because Grandma was welcoming, complimentary, generous with food, and a positive presence in his life. Unlike his mother, Grandma was jolly and permitted Jody great freedom. 5. Oliver's return caused excitement because he was adored by Grandma Hutto, Jody, and Penny. Since he only came home twice a year, his arrival was a special event. Also, everyone was anxious to hear about his exciting life at sea. 6. Jody worried that his participation in the fight would prevent him from visiting the Forresters again and thus keep him from seeing his friend Fodder-wing.

Chapters 14-16

Vocabulary: 1. b 2. d 3. a 4. a 5. d 6. b

Questions: 1. Ma wanted her son and husband to go out on a hunt again because she wanted them to track down the hogs and perhaps bring back other meat as well. This was so important to her that she was not concerned about a possible face off that might occur between the Forresters and her son and husband. 2. Penny shot the deer because he needed its organs to help draw the venomous blood from his snake bite. 3. Jody and Ma considered Buck a friend not only because he helped bring the doctor, but he also agreed to help the Baxters with farmwork until Penny recovered. 4. Once Penny was beginning to recover, he could not deny his son the offspring of the deer that had helped to save his life. When the doctor and the Forrester boys agreed, Ma alone could not refuse Jody his wish. 5. After working and living at the Baxters' farm for more than eight days, Buck became restless and felt the need to return home. He also feared that Fodder-wing was not well. 6. On the night that Buck had brought honey back to the Baxters' farm, a bear came prowling. Buck shot the bear for the Baxters so they would have meat and so it would not injure Jody's fawn.

Chapters 17-19

Vocabulary: Across — 1. apparition 5. belligerently 10. somnolent 11. mute; Down — 2. paradox 3. rank 4. zenith 6. ludicrous 7. covet 8. pungent 9. meager

Questions: 1. Since Penny's recovery was slow and intensive work fatigued him, Jody had to do most of the farmwork himself once Buck left. 2. Jody felt privileged because now he had a wonderful tale to tell, just as his father and the other men told to one another. 3. When Jody first learned of Fodder-wing's death, he denied the truth. It was not until he viewed the body that he understood death. He then sought solace in the affection of the fawn. Jody spent the night because the Baxters expected him, as Fodder-wing's only friend, to be present at the burial. Jody felt he owed this to his friend and to the Baxters since Buck had helped during his father's recuperation. 4. The Baxters were comforted by Penny knowing that he had survived the loss of so many children. It reminded them that "no man was spared." 5. The return of the Baxters' hogs along with a brood sow was the Forresters' peace offering. 6. Jody began to fear hunters targeting Flag by mistake. Penny tried to allay his son's fears by telling other adults nearby that Jody's fawn was a pet, not wild game. 7. The storm curtailed the Baxters' farm activities, leaving most of the livestock to fend for themselves and requiring a gathering of the nearly-ruined crops. The loss of much of their crop would represent a hardship for the Baxters.

Chapters 20-22

Vocabulary: 1. c 2. h 3. a 4. g 5. f 6. b 7. e 8. d; 1. refuge 2. sodden 3. unprecedented 4. privation 5. palatable 6. encounter 7. malodorous 8. transparent

Questions: 1. Buck, Mill-wheel, Penny, and Jody went off together to check on storm damage in their locale and to see if any people needed their help. Penny did not want Jody to bring the fawn along because their trip had a serious, not a recreational, purpose. 2. The Forresters shot any animal they found, but Penny only shot an animal for food at a time when the animal was fair game. Answers to the second part of the question will vary. 3. The storm had ravaged the land. Farmland was flooded and many animals were drowned. Water in rivers and ponds was polluted. 4. The men allowed Jody to take the first shot when a small group of bears appeared. They backed up his initial shot with additional shots. 5. The animals were dying of a plague that might have been caused by water contamination. Jody worried that Flag might succumb if he consumed contaminated water or plants. With the crops ruined by the storm and the animals dying of a plague, food would be scarce. 6. The Baxters killed their hogs for food before they were all taken by animals, such as bears, who were emboldened by the scarcity of prey. 7. The fawn had ravaged the sweet potatoes, one of the Baxters' only remaining food sources from the crop that had been decimated by the storm.

Chapters 23-25

Vocabulary: 1. c 2. b 3. d 4. a 5. c 6. a 7. d 8. b
Questions: 1. Although Penny had shot a wolf and dispersed the pack, the wolves had killed a heifer and would probably return for the rest of the livestock. As a pack, they posed a greater problem than single foraging animals. 2. The Forresters wanted to poison the wolf pack, but Penny opted for the less efficient, but more humane alternative of hunting and shooting the animals. Answers to the second part of the question will vary. 3. Jody was angry and hurt that Oliver, seeing a need to get away with Twink and away from his competition, Lem Forrester, had placed his romance over his friendship with Jody, leaving without a farewell. 4. The Forresters decided to hunt the remaining wolves when they became wary of the poisoned meat. 5. Birds, aquatic animals, and amphibians best survived the plague. 6. The Baxters went to Volusia to trade goods, venison, and bear for Christmas gifts for each other.

Chapters 26-28

Vocabulary: 1. harbinger 2. boisterous 3. whimper 4. imperceptible 5. impetus 6. lethargy 7. jovial
Questions: 1. Jody's mother cried with delight when Penny gave her the black alpaca. Answers to the second part of the question will vary, but should include the idea that this gift was a tangible representation of her husband's love and that gifts were a rare treat because the family had little money. 2. Penny felt it was more crucial for him to hunt down Slewfoot than it was to attend Christmas celebrations. Answers to the second part of the question will vary, but should include the idea that Ma Baxter had baked a special cake, had sewn new clothes for everyone, and was looking forward to her first festive Christmas in many years. 3. Penny was unable to shoot down the bear because by the time he was able to get through the swamp within shooting distance, the bear had crossed a creek too wide for the dogs to follow. 4. Nellie had inadvertently provided her cabin so that Jody and Penny could rest before continuing the hunt. She also gave them the use of her canoe so they could cross the creek. 5. Just when Penny and Jody thought they would have to walk to Fort Gates to get help in moving the dead bear, the Forresters came along on their horses and were willing to transport the animal. 6. Once the people calmed down after the Forresters' practical joke, Penny and Jody were treated like conquering heroes for killing the bear that had been ravaging the countryside.

Chapters 29-33

Vocabulary: 1. f 2. g 3. e 4. h 5. a 6. d 7. b 8. c; 1. cajoled 2. arduous 3. melancholy 4. incentive 5. lamented 6. din 7. impudent 8. plausible
Questions: 1. Flag had become less content in the shed, using every opportunity to slip free of his restraints. It became less appropriate to allow him in the house where he butted and bumped into everything he could. He no longer slept long hours and was becoming increasingly restless at night. 2. The destruction of the tobacco seed bed meant that the family would not have a money crop. 3. Jody was relieved when his parents decided to let him keep Flag if he planted more corn and built a high fence. Jody had expected them to make him get rid of Flag. 4. When Flag cleared the high fence that Jody built and ate the cornshoots, Jody's parents agreed that Flag had to be killed. It was clear that Penny had put off this decision until his family's food supply was endangered. Until then, he had argued with his wife and found ways for Jody to keep Flag. 5. Jody was disappointed because the

Forrester boys were away trading and could not help Jody with his plan to take Flag to Jacksonville. Also, the elder Forresters agreed with Jody's parents that Flag had to be shot. 6. Jody felt his father had betrayed him. After years of depending on his father for comfort and sympathy, Jody could not understand the rationale behind his father's decision to let Flag be shot. 7. While Jody was running away and had gone without food for many days, he came to understand that this was the excruciating hunger his parents feared when Flag had eaten the crops. 8. Jody felt a sudden need to rush home to see his father even though he feared he would not be wanted or that his father died.

NOTES: